I Know Someone with
Eczema

Vic Parker

www.raintreepublishers.co.uk
Visit our website to find out more information about Raintree books.

To order:

☎ Phone 0845 6044371

🖷 Fax +44 (0) 1865 312263

🖳 Email myorders@raintreepublishers.co.uk

Customers from outside the UK please telephone +44 1865 312262

Raintree is an imprint of Capstone Global Library Limited, a company incorporated in England and Wales having its registered office at 7 Pilgrim Street, London, EC4V 6LB – Registered company number: 6695582

Text © Capstone Global Library Limited 2011
First published in hardback in 2011
First published in paperback in 2012
The moral rights of the proprietor have been asserted.

Edited by Rebecca Rissman, Dan Nunn, and Catherine Veitch
Designed by Steve Mead and Joanna Hinton Malivoire
Picture research by Tracy Cummins
Originated by Capstone Global Library
Printed and bound in China by Leo Paper Products Ltd

ISBN 978 1 406 22079 7 (hardback)
15 14 13 12 11
10 9 8 7 6 5 4 3 2 1

ISBN 978 1 406 22353 8 (paperback)
16 15 14 13 12 11
10 9 8 7 6 5 4 3 2 1

British Library Cataloguing in Publication Data
Parker, Victoria.
I know someone with eczema. –
(Understanding health issues)
616.5'1-dc22
A full catalogue record for this book is available from the British Library.

Acknowledgements
We would like to thank the following for permission to reproduce photographs: Alamy pp. **4** (© Bubbles Photolibrary), **10** (© Axel Leschinski), **13** (© Olaf Doering), **18** (© Bubbles Photolibrary); Corbis pp. **5** (© Image Source), **6** (© Roy McMahon), **9** (© Corbis), **15** (© moodboard); Getty Images pp. **11** (Muntz), **16** (Alistair Berg), **17** (Michael Wildsmith), **20** (Roger Charity), **25** (C Flanigan/FilmMagic); istockphoto pp. **12** (© steve Wilson), **14** (© David Newton), **21** (© Carmen Martínez Banús), **23** (© Aldo Murillo), **27** (© Joshua Hodge Photography); Photo Researchers, Inc. pp. **7** (Dr P. Marazzi), **22** (Phanie); The Kobal Collection p. **24** (Paramount Pictures/ Warner Bros. Pictures).

Cover photograph of two girls riding piggyback reproduced with permission of istockphoto (© Rosemarie Gearhart).

We would like to thank Ashley Wolinski and Matthew Siegel for their invaluable help in the preparation of this book.

Every effort has been made to contact copyright holders of any material reproduced in this book. Any omissions will be rectified in subsequent printings if notice is given to the publisher.

All the Internet addresses (URLs) given in this book were valid at the time of going to press. However, due to the dynamic nature of the Internet, some addresses may have changed, or sites may have changed or ceased to exist since publication. While the author and publisher regret any inconvenience this may cause readers, no responsibility for any such changes can be accepted by either the author or the publisher.

Contents

Some words are printed in bold, **like this**. You can find out what they mean in the glossary.

Do you know someone with eczema?

Eczema is a medical **condition** which affects the skin. You may have a friend with eczema. People with eczema are affected in different ways.

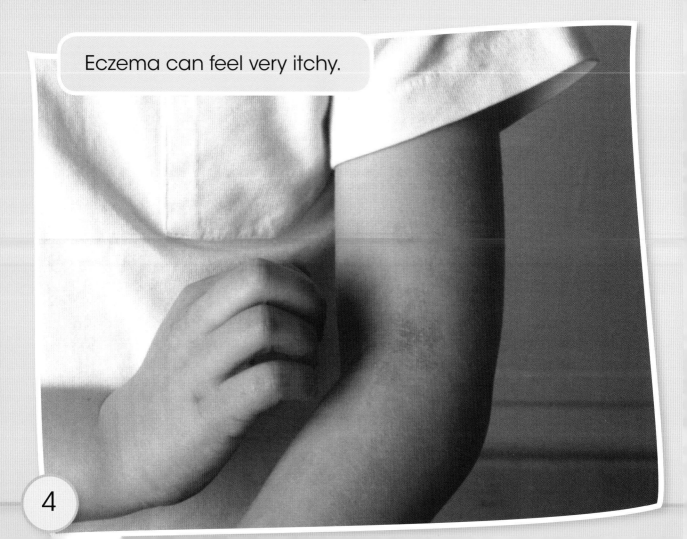

Eczema can feel very itchy.

Touching someone who has eczema will not mean you get it too.

A person can get eczema anywhere on their body, so you might be able to see that someone has it. But no matter how bad their eczema is, you cannot catch it.

What is eczema?

Strong sun can be harmful to skin cells.

Our skin is made up of millions of tiny **cells** that are too small to see. Some cells act like bricks, forming a cell wall on the outside of the body. Other cells act like soldiers, fighting off harmful things.

There are problems with these cells in the skin of someone with eczema. These problems cause the skin to become red and sore, or swollen.

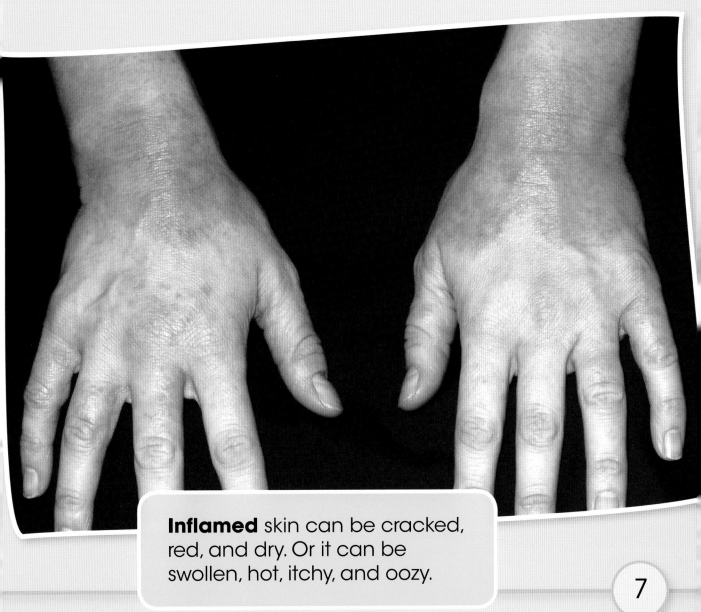

Inflamed skin can be cracked, red, and dry. Or it can be swollen, hot, itchy, and oozy.

What can make eczema worse?

Things that can make eczema worse	
Things that can dry out skin:	• soap • washing powder • hot water • cold, dry winter air.
Things that can irritate skin:	• perfumes • scented lotions • sweat • scratchy materials such as wool.

People can have eczema in patches or all over the body. It can be there all the time or it can come and go. One thing that can make it worse is **stress**.

Some people get eczema after their skin touches something that is not harmful to most people, like animal fur or dust. Some people get it after eating certain food, like cow's milk or wheat. We say this eczema is an **allergic reaction**.

Some people with eczema have to check food labels carefully.

9

Preventing eczema

People can try to stop their eczema by avoiding the things that make it worse. Some things, such as wearing woolly clothes, are much easier to avoid than others, such as grass **pollen**.

Avoiding the things that make eczema worse can feel frustrating and upsetting.

If a person's eczema gets worse in cold, dry air, play indoors with them on wintry days.

Other people can often help someone with eczema. For example, if someone shouldn't eat wheat, offer them rice cakes as a snack instead of a biscuit.

Treatments for eczema

People with eczema can use creams and lotions to help dry and itchy skin feel better. Doctors can also give them medicines to get rid of swelling.

When eczema is very bad, a bandage can be put on the skin after the cream has been rubbed in.

Some people's eczema is made better if they spend time under special lamps.

There are tablets, liquids, and creams that can help stop itching. People who have very bad eczema can try a **treatment** using special lamps to help clear up the **condition**.

Who gets eczema?

Anyone of any age can get eczema. It can start at any time. However, children usually get it before they are five and many grow out of it by their teens.

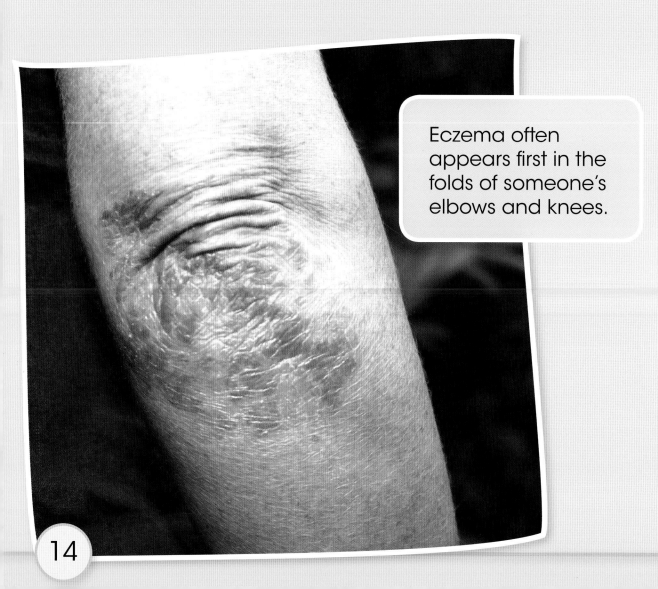

Eczema often appears first in the folds of someone's elbows and knees.

Children who have eczema often have asthma or hay fever, too.

Many adults have eczema. Most people with eczema have other family members who have it, or they have family members who have **hay fever** or **asthma**.

Living with eczema

People who have eczema can sometimes feel embarrassed by it. This is often true when their eczema is where other people can see it, such as on their face.

Eczema can make people very shy and unconfident.

Friends can support and help someone with eczema.

But someone with eczema should not feel shy or nervous. Many people have the **condition**. There is no reason why someone with eczema should not do things with everyone else.

Coping with itching

Eczema can itch a lot. It can sometimes be so bad that people can't sleep and feel very tired the next day. People usually feel like they need to scratch, but scratching only makes eczema worse.

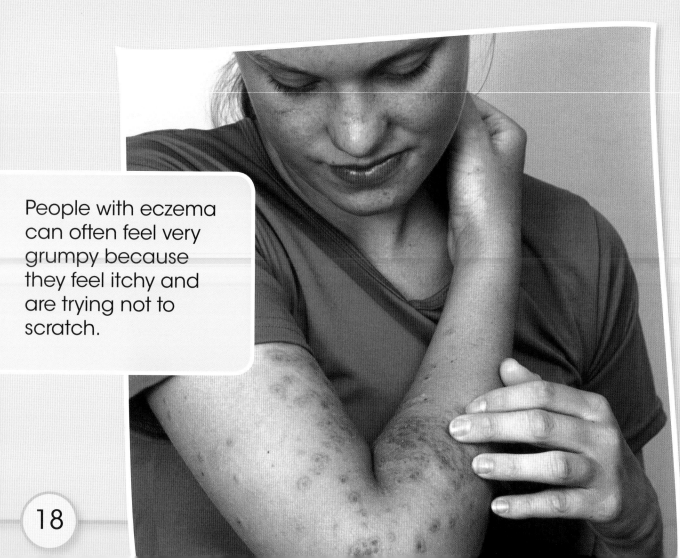

People with eczema can often feel very grumpy because they feel itchy and are trying not to scratch.

Here are some things which can help people with eczema deal with itching:

- don't spend too long in the bath or shower as hot water makes itching worse

- avoid soap and perfumes, because these can dry skin

- pat, don't rub, with a towel

- use creams and lotions often

- wear loose clothing made of soft, natural fibres, like cotton

- keep nails short as scratching with long nails does more damage.

Exercise and sport

Sport can make skin with eczema worse if it gets hot and sweaty, or if the air is cold and dry. Swimming in a pool can make eczema worse because of the chemicals in it that keep the water clean.

People who have eczema should shower straight after they swim and then rub on a lotion.

Golf, archery, and yoga are all good sport choices for people with eczema.

However, people with eczema do not have to miss out. Wearing loose cotton clothes and showering straight after exercise can help. So can taking part in activities where the skin keeps cool.

Growing older with eczema

As children get older they often grow out of eczema, but many teenagers and adults do have the **condition**. It can make people feel very shy around friends or when they are at work.

Girls and women can buy special make-up which doesn't harm eczema.

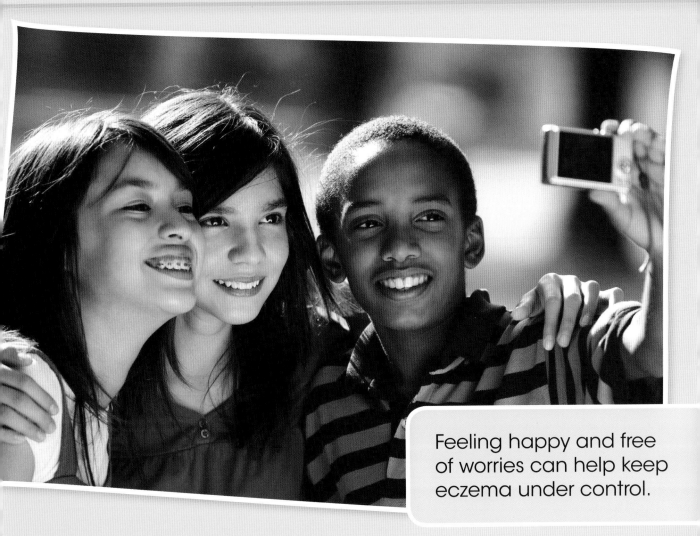

Feeling happy and free of worries can help keep eczema under control.

Friends can be very important in helping people live with their eczema. Everyone feels happy and forgets things that trouble them when they share fun times with friends.

Famous people

Film star Brad Pitt once had eczema all over his body. His skin was **irritated** by all the make-up he had to wear during the filming of *The Curious Case of Benjamin Button*.

In *Benjamin Button*, Brad Pitt had to have lots of ageing make-up put on him!

LeAnn Rimes is a famous pop and country singer.

Singer-songwriter LeAnn Rimes has had eczema since she was two years old, but she hasn't let it stop her. She has often topped the charts and appeared in magazines and advertisements all around the world.

Being a good friend

There are many ways you can be a good friend to someone with eczema, such as:

- stick up for your friend if others tease them
- put people right if they think that eczema is catching
- stay behind with your friend if they have to put on eczema creams.

We all have different bodies and different personalities.

Living with eczema can be difficult at times. But we are all different in many ways. A good friend will like us just as we are.

Eczema – facts and fiction

Facts

- There are many different types of eczema and each one can be mild or **severe**.

- Eczema is becoming more and more common.

- Eczema is also sometimes called **dermatitis**.

Fiction

(?) Eczema is caused because a person is unclean.

WRONG! Anyone can get eczema, at any time. It has nothing to do with being unclean.

(?) Eczema leaves permanent **scarring**.

WRONG! Eczema does not usually give people scars forever. Some medicines can change the skin colour, but this soon wears off.

Glossary

allergic reaction when someone's body reacts badly to something he or she touches, breathes, eats, or drinks

asthma illness that makes breathing difficult

cell smallest unit that makes up living things

condition something that affects the way some parts of the body work

dermatitis another name for eczema

hay fever allergy to pollen, which makes a person sneeze, have watery or itchy eyes, and a runny nose

inflamed red and swollen skin

irritate make itchy

pollen fine powder made by certain plants

scarring have permanent marks on the skin

severe extremely bad

stress worrying too much

treatment medical care

Find out more

Books to read

Rachel Has Eczema (Dr Spot's Casebook), Jenny Leigh (Red Kite Books, 2003)

Skin (Amazing Human Body), Lorrie Klosterman (Marshall Cavendish Children's Books, 2008)

Why do I get sunburn? And other questions about skin (Body Matters), Angela Royston (Heinemann Library, 2002)

Websites

http://kidshealth.org/kid/ill_injure/aches/ eczema.html
Learn all about eczema on this website.

Index